My Word Bank

Name: _____

School: _____

Class: _____

Contents

about

above

accident

achieve

across

admire

aeroplane

after

afternoon

again

alligator

almost

along

always

angry

animal

another

answer

any

anybody

anyone

anything

around

asleep

assembly

ate

away

Aa

again about another always above

angry angel along alligator

babies	brought	
banana	build	
barbecue	buy	
beach	by	
bear		
beautiful		
because		
before		
began		
behind		
believe		
belong		
between		
bicycle		
birthday		
bought		
brake		
break		
breakfast		
breath		
breathe		
broken		
brother		

be before babies
buy because brake

Bb

broken by beautiful breakfast

cake	course	
call	cousin	
came	cried	
can't	cry	
catch		
caught		
chair		
change		
children		
chocolate		
city		
classroom		
clean		
climb		
close		
clothes		
colour		
come		
coming		
computer		
could		
couldn't		
country		

 My Word Bank   www.prim-ed.com   Prim-Ed Publishing®

Cc

can't come could can classroom call

children caught cry colour

dance	drought	
dangerous	dry	
date	during	
dear		
decided		
dentist		
didn't		
different		
digital		
dinner		
disappear		
disaster		
dirty		
does		
doesn't		
doing		
done		
don't		
down		
dream		
drink		
drive		
dropped		

don't dear done
does disaster drink

Dd

decide dream drive
disappear

each	everywhere	
early	excellent	
earth	exciting	
easy	explain	
eat	explanation	
edge		
education		
either		
electricity		
else		
email		
empty		
enjoy		
enough		
enter		
enthusiastic		
envelope		
environment		
estimate		
evening		
every		
everyone		
everything		

each every earth
enough either explain

Ee

exciting edge eat
everyone

face	full	
fall	funny	
family		
farm		
fast		
father		
favourite		
few		
fight		
finally		
find		
finish		
first		
floor		
flower		
for		
forget		
found		
four		
friend		
frightened		
from		
front		

 www.prim-ed.com Prim-Ed Publishing®

fast fall **favourite** from first face

Ff

father forget flower family

game	ground	
garden	group	
gave	grow	
gel	guess	
gentle		
germ		
getting		
giant		
girl		
give		
glad		
glasses		
glide		
glue		
goes		
going		
gone		
goodbye		
government		
grab		
grass		
grate		
great		

glue **grow** give great
girl **government**

Gg

goodbye gel gave
getting

hairy	how	
half	hungry	
handle	hurry	
happened	hurt	
happy		
hard		
have		
haven't		
having		
heard		
heart		
height		
hello		
help		
her		
hero		
him		
hold		
holidays		
home		
honey		
hope		
house		

My Word Bank   www.prim-ed.com   Prim-Ed Publishing®

hero   house **hurt**

help **happened** how

Hh

holidays have her
hungry

Prim-Ed Publishing®   www.prim-ed.com   **My Word Bank**   19

iceblock	its	
ice-cream	it's	
idea	itself	
identify		
idiom		
idol		
ill		
image		
important		
industry		
insect		
inside		
instead		
instruction		
interesting		
international		
invention		
invisible		
invitation		
iron		
island		
isn't		
itchy		

idea itchy insect
its ice-cream isn't

Ii

island idol instead
invisible

jacket	junk	
jaw	Jupiter	
jazz	jury	
jealous	just	
jeans		
jelly		
jellyfish		
jetty		
jewellery		
jigsaw		
join		
joint		
joke		
jolly		
jolt		
journal		
journey		
joy		
juice		
juggle		
jumper		
junior		
jungle		

jeans **juice** joke
jaw **journey** jigsaw

Jj

Jupiter jungle jazz
jewellery

keen

keep

key

keyboard

khaki

kick

kind

king

kitchen

kite

kitten

knead

knee

kneel

knelt

knew

knife

knight

knitting

knock

knot

know

knowledge

www.prim-ed.com Prim-Ed Publishing®

key know **knife** knock
knowledge knew

Kk

kitchen knife kneel
kitten kite

lady	lose	
large	lost	
last	loud	
late	love	
laugh	lucky	
lay		
lazy		
leaf		
learn		
leave		
left		
legend		
library		
light		
lightning		
like		
listen		
little		
live		
lollipop		
long		
look		
loose		

lose library legend
learn listen loose

Ll

lightning little love
laugh

machine	Mr	
made	Mrs	
magazine	much	
magic	music	
main	myself	
make		
making		
meat		
meet		
message		
midnight		
might		
mischief		
mistake		
money		
monster		
morning		
mosquito		
most		
mother		
mountain		
mouse		
move		

make music much
Mr mountain meet

Mm

morning might Mrs
mistake

nail	noticeable	
name	nuisance	
naughty	number	
near	nurse	
necessary		
neighbour		
nephew		
never		
new		
newspaper		
next		
nice		
niece		
night		
no		
no-one		
nobody		
noise		
none		
noodles		
normal		
nothing		
notice		

www.prim-ed.com Prim-Ed Publishing®

never next noise
name nuisance new

Nn

nobody night none
neither

object	owe	
occasion	own	
occupy	oxygen	
ocean		
o'clock		
octopus		
odd		
of		
off		
offered		
often		
once		
one		
only		
open		
opinion		
opportunity		
opposite		
other		
otherwise		
our		
outside		
over		

owe **odd** **other**
our **outside** only

Oo

opinion **over** one
otherwise

paper	promise	
parade	pull	
party	put	
past	putting	
peace	pyjamas	
pencil		
people		
person		
phone		
photograph		
picture		
piece		
place		
plastic		
play		
playground		
please		
police		
pool		
potato		
pretend		
pretty		
probably		

peace past play
piece probably pull

Pp

pyjamas pool put
please

quality

quantity

queen

question

queue

quick

quiet

quit

quite

quiz

queen **quick** quickly
quit **quality** quantity

Qq

question quite quiz
quiet

race	room	
radio	rough	
rain	round	
rainbow	rubber	
raincoat	ruler	
rare		
rather		
raw		
read		
ready		
really		
reason		
receive		
remember		
reply		
restaurant		
rhyme		
rhythm		
right		
road		
robot		
rocket		
rollerskates		

www.prim-ed.com Prim-Ed Publishing®

rather **read** **radio**
rare **rainbow** rough

Rr

remember **road**
raw

said	story	
sandwich	successfully	
saw	suddenly	
school	suppose	
scissors	sure	
sea		
secret		
see		
sentence		
separate		
shall		
share		
she		
shoe		
should		
sister		
small		
snow		
someone		
something		
sometimes		
special		
squeeze		

www.prim-ed.com Prim-Ed Publishing®

sister start sleep
saw scissors small

Ss

suppose sure see
separate

take	tomorrow	_____
talk	tonight	_____
taste	too	_____
teacher	trouble	_____
telephone	truly	_____
television	turn	_____
terrible		_____
terrific	_____	_____
that's	_____	_____
their	_____	_____
there	_____	_____
these	_____	_____
they	_____	_____
they're	_____	_____
thing	_____	_____
thirsty	_____	_____
those	_____	_____
thought	_____	_____
threw	_____	_____
through	_____	_____
throw	_____	_____
together	_____	_____
told		

their they're that's
there tomorrow too

Tt

teacher told talk
take

ugly

umbrella

umpire

uncle

under

underneath

understand

unit

universe

unless

unnecessary

upright

upstairs

urgent

use

useful

usual

uncle unless under
ugly umbrella usual

Uu

upstairs upper unit
urgent

vacuum

valley

value

vanish

vary

vase

vegetable

vehicle

venomous

very

vicious

victory

video

view

violin

visit

visual

voice

volcano

vote

voice **view** vehicle
vary **venomous** very

Vv

vacuum value vase
victory

walk	window	
want	wish	
warm	without	
was	woman	
wasn't	women	
watch	wonderful	
water	world	
way	would	
wear	wouldn't	
weather		
weekend		
weird		
were		
we're		
what		
when		
where		
which		
while		
whisper		
who		
whole		
why		

were when wrong
was wonderful why

Ww

whisper what while
would

X-ray

xylophone

X-ray

Xx

xylophone

yacht

yard

yawn

year

yell

yes

yesterday

yoga

yoghurt

you

young

your

yourself

youth

yoyo

yacht **your** you're
year **yourself** yawn

Yy

yesterday yes
yoyo

zebra

zero

zest

zigzag

zip

zinc

zodiac

zoo

zoom

zone

zip
zest zodiac zebra zoo

Zz

zigzag zero zinc
zone

Words to do with Time

after	next	while
ago	now	year
always	o'clock	yesterday
as	often	yet
before	present	
century	presently	
day	recently	
decade	second	
during	seldom	
every	since	
first	sometimes	
hour	soon	
immediately	still	
last	then	
lately	today	
later	tomorrow	
millennium	tonight	
minute	until	
moment	usually	
month	week	
never	when	

Months of the Year

January

February

March

April

May

June

July

August

September

October

November

December

Seasons

spring

summer

autumn

winter

Days of the Week

Sunday

Monday

Tuesday

Wednesday

Thursday

Friday

Saturday

Me

Parts of the Body

ankle

arm

back

blood

bones

brain

buttocks

cheeks

chest

chin

ear

elbow

eye

eyebrow

eyelashes

eyelid

face

finger

fingernail

hair

head

heart

heel

intestines

kidney

knee

knuckle

liver

lung

mouth

neck

nose

nostril

shoulder

stomach

taste buds

teeth

thigh

thumb

toe

toenail

tongue

veins

wrist

Feelings

enthusiastic

frightened

happy

amazed · hesitant

annoyed · insulted

bored · interested

calm · irritated

cheerful · joyous

comfortable · lonely

concerned · miserable

content · nervous

courageous · offended

curious · relaxed

delighted · satisfied

determined · scared

disappointed · surprised

disgusted · suspicious

disinterested · tense

distressed · terrified

distrustful · thankful

doubtful · thrilled

eager

embarrassed

Maths

angle	opposites	
area	ordinal	**Operations**
array	perimeter	
average	place value	addition
capacity	polygon	division
centimetre	right angle	multiplication
decimal	rotation	subtraction
estimate	tangram	
factor	tessellation	
fraction	vertical	
gram	volume	
horizontal		
hundredth		
kilogram (kg)		
kilometre (km)		
line		
litre (L)		
mass		
millilitre (mL)		
multiple		
negative number		

Shapes

cone

cube

cylinder

hexagon

octagon

parallelogram

pentagon

rectangle

square

trapezium

triangle

_____

_____

_____

Ordinal Numbers

first

second

third

fourth

fifth

sixth

seventh

eighth

ninth

tenth

eleventh

twelfth

thirteenth

fourteenth

fifteenth

sixteenth

seventeenth

eighteenth

nineteenth

twentieth

thirtieth

fortieth

fiftieth

sixtieth

seventieth

eightieth

ninetieth

hundredth

thousandth

millionth

_____

_____

_____

_____

_____

_____

_____

_____

_____

_____

Words other than...

said

added
agreed
announced
answered
asked
called
commented
complained
cried
described
drawled
explained
expressed
fumed
laughed
mentioned
mumbled
ordered

pleaded
ranted
screamed
shouted
sobbed
stammered
stated
suggested
uttered
whispered
yelled

went

crawled
crept
danced
dawdled
drove
flew
hopped
skipped
strutted
tiptoed
trudged
walked
wandered

My Word Bank www.prim-ed.com Prim-Ed Publishing®

good

brilliant

excellent

exceptional

fantastic

fine

first-class

first-rate

great

marvellous

splendid

super

superb

valuable

wonderful

worthy

_____

_____

_____

_____

big

colossal

enormous

extensive

gigantic

huge

hulking

immense

jumbo

king-sized

mammoth

massive

thundering

vast

whopping

_____

_____

_____

_____

_____

small

baby

little

microscopic

mini

miniature

minuscule

minute

pocket-sized

short

shrimp

slight

teensy

tiny

_____

_____

_____

_____

_____

Sport

athletics

badminton

baseball

basketball

bowls

cricket

diving

football

Gaelic football

golf

hockey

hurling

netball

rugby

softball

surfing

swimming

tennis

water polo

Colours

amber	grey	viridian
apple green	indigo	yellow
apricot	jade	zinc
aqua	khaki	_____
black	lavender	_____
brown	lilac	_____
buttercup	magenta	_____
caramel	maroon	_____
charcoal grey	mauve	_____
chocolate	mustard	_____
claret	olive green	_____
copper	orange	_____
cream	pale green	_____
crimson	pearl	_____
dark brown	pink	_____
dark green	salmon pink	_____
emerald green	scarlet	_____
fawn	silver	_____
gold	terracotta	_____
grape	turquoise	_____
green	violet	_____

Celebrations

April Fool's Day

Birthdays

Buddhist New Year

Chinese New Year

Christmas

Diwali

Easter

Father's Day

Feast of Eid

Good Friday

Halloween

Hanukkah

May Day

Mother's Day

New Year's Eve

Passover

Ramadan

St Andrew's Day

St David's Day

St George's Day

St Patrick's Day

Valentine's Day

History and Geography

ancient

Aztecs

Celts

century

climate

community

Egyptians

environment

globe

Greeks

past

Romans

society

sustainable

Vikings

weather

Countries

Afghanistan	Finland	Kuwait
Argentina	France	Laos
Australia	Germany	Latvia
Austria	Ghana	Lebanon
Bangladesh	Greece	Libya
Belgium	Hungary	Luxembourg
Bolivia	Iceland	Macedonia
Bosnia	India	Madagascar
Botswana	Indonesia	Malaysia
Brazil	Iran	Maldives
Brunei	Iraq	Malta
Cambodia	Ireland	Mauritania
Canada	Israel	Mauritius
Chile	Italy	Mexico
Croatia	Jamaica	Monaco
Cuba	Japan	Mongolia
Denmark	Jordan	Morocco
East Timor	Kazakhstan	Mozambique
Ecuador	Kenya	Namibia
Egypt	Korea, North	Nepal
Ethiopia	Korea, South	Netherlands

New Zealand	Spain	Venezuela
Nicaragua	Sri Lanka	Vietnam
Nigeria	Sudan	Yemen
Norway	Sweden	Yugoslavia
Oman	Switzerland	Zaire
Pakistan	Taiwan	Zambia
Panama	Tanzania	Zimbabwe
Papua New Guinea	Thailand	
Peru	Tonga	
Philippines	Trinidad and	
Poland	Tobago	
Portugal	Tunisia	
Romania	Turkey	
Russia	Uganda	
Rwanda	Ukraine	
Samoa	United Arab	
Saudi Arabia	Emirates	
Singapore	United Kingdom	
Slovakia	United States	
Slovenia	of America	
Solomon Islands	Uruguay	
Somalia	Uzbekistan	
South Africa	Vatican City	

Spelling Rules

'fairy e' changes short vowel sounds into long vowel sounds.

For example:

hop - hope

not - note

tub - tube

'q' is usually followed by 'u'.

For example:

queen

quite

quarter

quiet

'f', 'l' and 's' are doubled at the end of most one-syllable words.

For example:

ball

stuff

boss

Words that don't follow this rule are:

of   gas   was   bus

When 'ie' says 'ee' then 'i' comes before 'e' except after 'c'.

For example:

'ie'	thief	belief	chief	piece
'ei'	receive	ceiling		

Words that don't follow this rule are:

weird   seize   weir   counterfeit

Mnemonics may help you remember how to spell some words.

For example:

loose **and** lose

Remember–Loose has two 'o's as in tooth. L**oo**se t**oo**th.

forest

Remember–The word 'tree' has one 'r' and so does the word 'fo**r**est'.

principal **and** principle

Remember–The princi**pal** is your pal.

current **and** currant

Remember–Ants like curr**ants**.

here **and** hear

Remember–We h**ear** with our ear

Notes

Prim-Ed Publishing®